Who am I

I am not what they say I am

Values / Goals

Confessions

TABLE OF CONTENTS

WHO AM I

Genesis 2:22-24
22 Then the LORD God made a woman from the rib he had taken out of the man, and he brought her to the man.
23 The man said, "This is now bone of my bones and fles of my flesh; she shall be called 'woman', for she was taken out of man."
24 That is why a man leaves his father and mother and is united to his wife, and they become one flesh.

Genesis 1:27 So God created man in His own image; in the image of God He created him; male and female He created them.

1 Peter 2:9
But you are a chosen race, a royal priesthood, a holy nation, a people for God's own possession, you may proclaim the excellence of him who called you out of darkness into his marvelous light:

Who are you? Ask yourself that question, Who am I? Take time to write here who you think you are or how you see yourself.

LOVED

_____
_____
_____
_____
_____
_____
_____
_____
_____
_____

VALUED

WHO AM I

Then asking yourself "who am I " often times we start to describe our title, a cheerleader, track star an artist etc. But is that who you really are? No, you are more than a title or label. You are God's beautiful creation. Customized by God created for great things.

Was it hard for you to describe yourself or answer the question "Who am I", why do you think that is?

CHOSEN

WHO AM I

But if I asked you to describe a friend or a celebrity like Cardi B, Beyonce, Ariana Grande or asked you who she is you would have so much to say. Why is that? All based on who you think they are. We should always be able to describe ourselves more highly then anyone else. Why? Because we should love ourselves more. See ourselves better.

When you know who you are you tend to know what you want or where you are going.

Take time to write down where you see yourself when you are 20, 30, 40, etc. Write down what you want in life, the job you want, the school you want to attend, or any business you want to start.

_____

_____

_____

_____

_____

_____

_____

_____

_____

_____

_____

_____

_____

FORGIVEN

Take time to write down what you think it takes to get there.

BEAUTIFUL

I am chosen

Jeremiah 29:11

" Before I formed you in the womb, I knew you (and approved of you as My chosen instrument). And before you were born I consecrated you (to Myself as My own); I have appointed you as a phrophet to the nations."

I am loved

Romans 5:8

" God shows his love for us in that while we were still sinners. Christ died for us.

I am forgiven

Isaiah 43:25-26 NIV

"I, even I, am he who blots out your transgressions, for my own sake, and remembers your sins no more. 26 Review the past for me, let us argue the matter together: state the case for your innocence.

YOU ARE CHOSEN

THERE IS NOTHING YOU CAN DO TO SEPERATE HIS LOVE FROM YOU.

I AM NOT WHAT THEY SAY I AM ...

We know that things are classified by thier characteristics, what they display. If someone was to place a label on you, what would they see? Where would they place you? What do you display in school, at home, around friends, in church or public? Are you the same or do you tend to fit into your surroundings.

Do you allow what others think to dictate your life, looks or friends? Are what other people think of you or your looks, clothes, job, etc important enough that you change to be accepted?

Take time to write down negative labels that people have called you below.

_____
_____
_____
_____
_____
_____
_____
_____
_____
_____
_____

IDENTITY

Now say this "I am not what they say I am"

Shine like a diamond

I AM BEAUTIFUL ...

When it comes to labels you can always remove them, and put the correct label or wear the right identity. If you have been told that you will not accomplish anything, or that you are a failure, or not attractive, not smart enough, a looser, a mistake etc, I don't care what it is ... it is a lie! Take that label off and replace it with this... say it to yourself... or create your identity.

I am somebody	I was made for a great purpose	I am beautiful
I am smart	I am needed	I am full of life
I am loved	I am talented	I am full of life
I am priceless	I am strong	I am balanced
I am unstoppable		

I am free to be exactly what God created me to be and nothing can stop me!

STRONG

I AM ...
FREE
FREE TO BE ME
I AM UNIQUE
I AM BEAUTIFUL
I AM STRONG

WHAT ASPIRATIONS DO YOU THINK ABOUT THE MOST.. WHAT DO YOU DREAM ABOUT TODAY...

Think about those things you "could do" list them here.

1. _____
2. _____
3. _____
4. _____
5. _____
6. _____
7. _____
8. _____

Think about those things you "yearn about doing" list them here.

1. _____
2. _____
3. _____
4. _____
5. _____
6. _____
7. _____
8. _____

What obstacles are keeping you from doing it?

1. _____
2. _____
3. _____
4. _____
5. _____
7. _____
8. _____

What can you do differently?

1. _____
2. _____
3. _____
4. _____
6. _____
7. _____
8. _____

DREAM

WHAT DO YOU VALUE THE MOST?

val·ue
'valyoo/
noun
noun: value; plural noun: values

1. the regard that something is held to deserve; the importance, worth, or usefulness of something.
2. consider (someone or something) to be important or beneficial; have a high opinion of.

What do you value? What are somethings that mean the world to you, that you have to have or accomplish. It keeps you awake sometimes, you dream of it? List 10 things you value or want in life?

1. _____
2. _____
3. _____
4. _____
5. _____
6. _____
7. _____
8. _____
9. _____
10. _____

WORTH

GOALS

What are your goals ? List 5

1. _____

2. _____

3. _____

4. _____

5. _____

FOCUS

You can have it!

What are some things that will keep you from achieving them?

WINNING

What will you do differently to achieve them now?

PLAN

Now take time to write down how you plan to accomplish any of those things. Pick one that matters to you most and start with it first.

BUILD

CONFIDENCE

WHAT IS CONFIDENCE

con·fi·dence
/ˈkänfədəns/
noun

Noun: confidence
the felling or belief that one can rely on someone or something; firm trust, that state of feeling certain about the truth of something.

Is confidence visible?

BUILD

I am powerful

I am loved

I am accepted

I am beautiful

I am strong

I am gifted

I am chosen and equipped for anything and equal to anything

I overcome all and anything my hands touch is successful

You can do it!

CONFESSIONS

I am unstoppable

I am unique because there is no one else like me

I am destined for greatness

CONFESSIONS

You can do it!

Today is the beginning of my destiny, I declare and decree that I will fulfill all that God has called me to be, I have great gifts on the inside of me. I start each day with a sound mind and positive thoughts that I will accomplish all that I have set in my heart to do, today is filled with creative ideas and strategies of success. Every where I go today I will have joy, peace, favor and protection. Nothing can stop me but me, and since I am determined to succeed I shall not fail. I am the change that is needed in this earth. You can do it!

CONFESSIONS

Notes

You are capable!

Notes

THOUGHTS

You are capable!

She Priceless

CONFESSIONS

www.ingramcontent.com/pod-product-compliance
Lightning Source LLC
Chambersburg PA
CBHW061754290426
44108CB00029B/2994